Wainwright's Destructible Colourable Flashcardable Doodle Quotation Guide to Power and Conflict: The AQA GCSE Poetry Anthology

Quotations chosen and drawn by Edward Wainwright

ISBN: 9781694804402

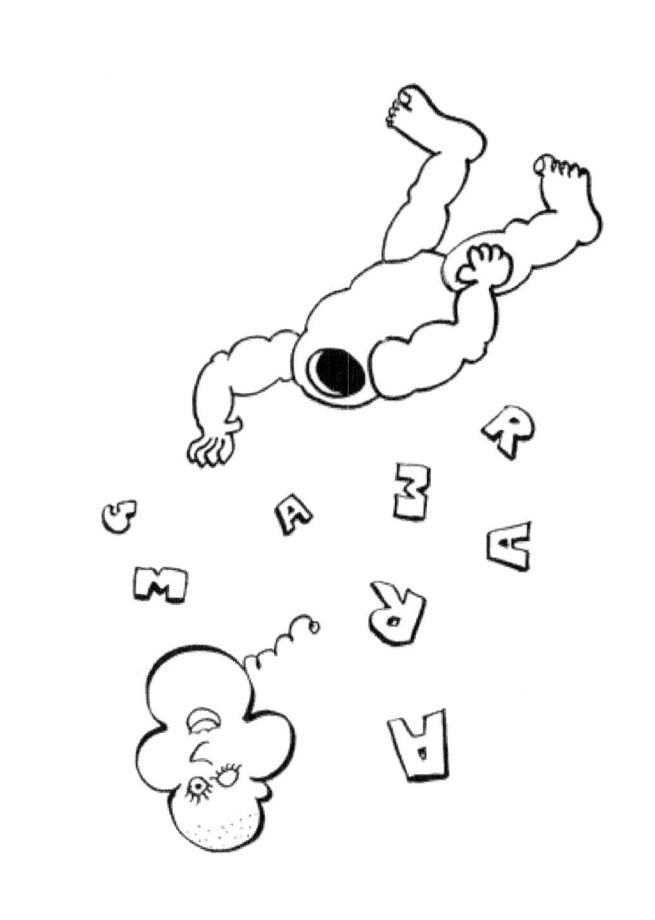

How to Abuse This Very Precious Book

This book is meant to help you to remember useful quotations so that you can use them in your exam. To do that you can abuse this book however you like — but here are some ideas:

1. Where there are already doodles, colour them in — it's a relaxing thing to do when you've no brain left for other revision.

2. If you think a quotation is very important, tear it out of the book and stick it up somewhere you'll see it often. Scatter them around the house to delight your family.

3. Share your beautiful or hilarious doodles online — your friends need them!

Can't draw? Don't worry! There are some memorably terrible doodles in here — the important part is that they're memorable and help you to learn the quotations. Draw, colour, share with your friends.

Don't forget to use your copy of the anthology with this book. Also, use a dictionary or the internet to look up any unfamiliar words and when you've done that label them, otherwise you'll look upon the exam writers' works and despair.

Finally, a slash / indicates a line break within a poem — they matter!

FLASHCARD

TEAR THIS PAGE OUT, FILL THIS SIDE IN AND BINGO! ~~~~~~ A FABULOUS FLASHCARD.

WRITE THE NUMBERS OF QUOTATIONS WHICH LINK TO THIS ONE HERE ↘

THIS QUOTATION IS ~~

ONE P~

_____

ANOTHER

_____

THE WORD KEY WORD

IS _____

~N HERE- MAKE THE SAME

Each flashcard includes a column for you to write the number of other quotations which compare well with the one on the flashcard. The comparison could be thematic- female power, for example - or it could be technical - perhaps both quotations are similes. The comparisons are important, though, so use the column!

·HIS MAKE YOU FEEL?

HOW WOULD OTHER AUDIENCES FEEL?

ASK: HOW DOES THIS LINK TO CONTEXT?

"I met a traveller from an antique land."

FLASHCARD

TEAR THIS PAGE OUT, FILL THIS SIDE IN AND BINGO! YOU HAVE A FABULOUS FLASHCARD.

WRITE THE NUMBERS OF QUOTATIONS WHICH LINK TO THIS ONE HERE ↘

THIS QUOTATION IS FROM
_____ .

ONE POETIC TECHNIQUE USED IS

_____ .

ANOTHER POETIC TECHNIQUE USED IS

_____ .

THE WORD CLASS OF THE KEY WORD "_____"

IS _____ .

WRITE THE QUOTATION HERE - MAKE SURE IT IS EXACTLY THE SAME AS IT IS ON THE OTHER SIDE!

ASK: HOW DOES THIS MAKE YOU FEEL?
ASK: HOW WOULD OTHER AUDIENCES FEEL?
ASK: HOW DOES THIS LINK TO CONTEXT?

MY NAME IS OZYMANDIAS, KING OF KINGS: LOOK ON MY WORKS, YE MIGHTY, AND DESPAIR!

"Nothing beside remains."

FLASHCARD

TEAR THIS PAGE OUT, FILL THIS SIDE IN AND BINGO! YOU HAVE A FABULOUS FLASHCARD.

WRITE THE NUMBERS OF QUOTATIONS WHICH LINK TO THIS ONE HERE ↓

THIS QUOTATION IS FROM

_____.

ONE POETIC TECHNIQUE USED IS

_____.

ANOTHER POETIC TECHNIQUE USED IS

_____.

THE WORD CLASS OF THE KEY WORD "_____"

IS _____.

WRITE THE QUOTATION HERE - MAKE SURE IT IS EXACTLY THE SAME AS IT IS ON THE OTHER SIDE!

ASK: HOW DOES THIS MAKE YOU FEEL?
ASK: HOW WOULD OTHER AUDIENCES FEEL?
ASK: HOW DOES THIS LINK TO CONTEXT?

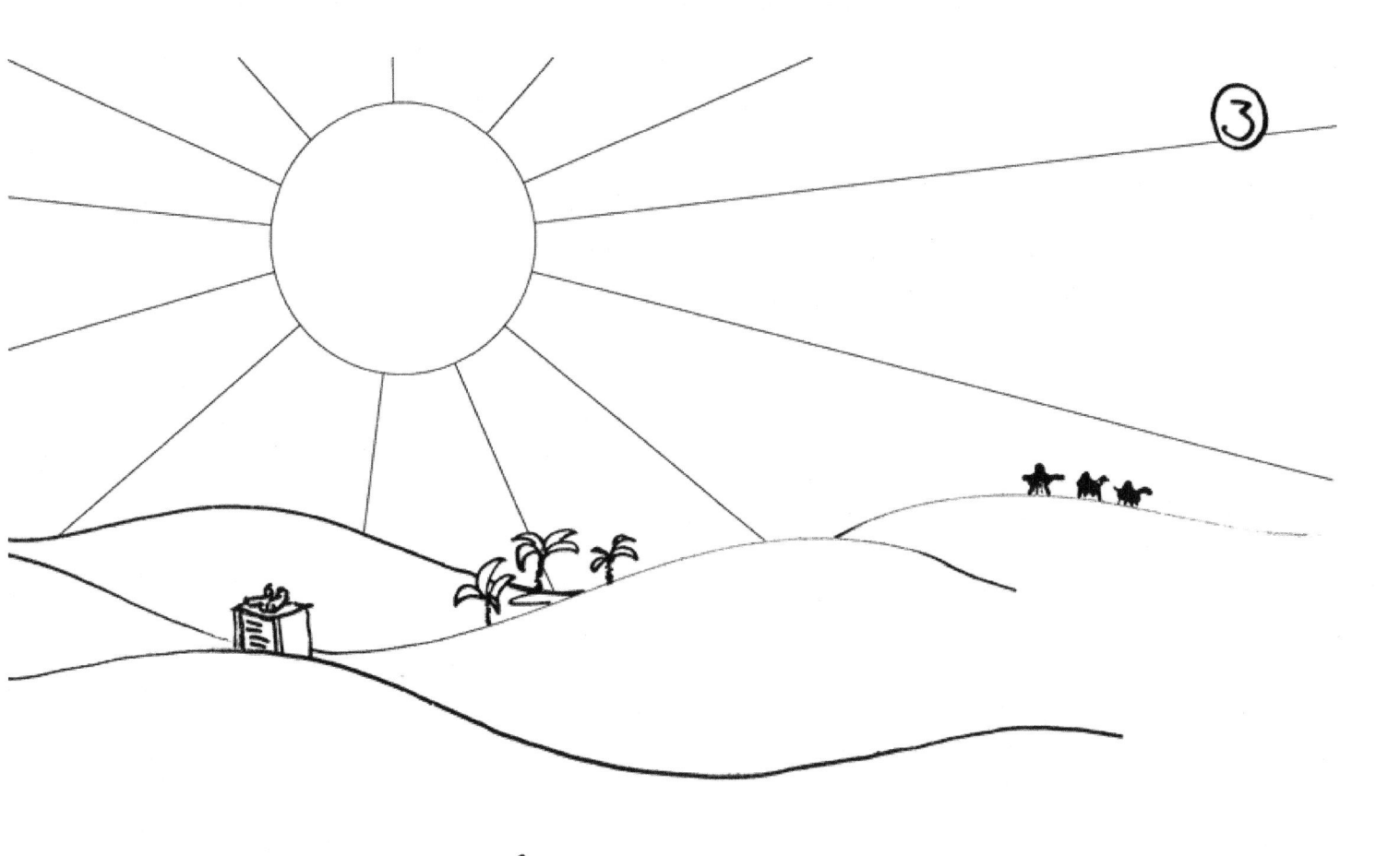

"The lone and level sands stretch far away."

FLASHCARD

TEAR THIS PAGE OUT, FILL THIS SIDE IN AND BINGO! YOU HAVE A FABULOUS FLASHCARD.

WRITE THE NUMBERS OF QUOTATIONS WHICH LINK TO THIS ONE HERE ↓

THIS QUOTATION IS FROM
_____.

ONE POETIC TECHNIQUE USED IS

_____.

ANOTHER POETIC TECHNIQUE USED IS

_____.

THE WORD CLASS OF THE KEY WORD "_____"

IS _____.

WRITE THE QUOTATION HERE— MAKE SURE IT IS EXACTLY THE SAME AS IT IS ON THE OTHER SIDE!

ASK: HOW DOES THIS MAKE YOU FEEL?
ASK: HOW WOULD OTHER AUDIENCES FEEL?
ASK: HOW DOES THIS LINK TO CONTEXT?

Pick your own quotation... (4)

...and do a doodle to suit it.

FLASHCARD

Tear this page out, fill this side in and bingo! You have a fabulous flashcard.

Write the numbers of quotations which link to this one here ↓

This quotation is from

_____ .

One poetic technique used is

_____ .

Another poetic technique used is

_____ .

The word class of the key word "_____" is _____ .

Write the quotation here- make sure it is exactly the same as it is on the other side!

ASK: How does this make you feel?
ASK: How would other audiences feel?
ASK: How does this link to context?

⑤

"Mark in every face I meet / Marks of weakness, Marks of woe."

FLASHCARD

Tear this page out, fill this side in and bingo! You have a fabulous flashcard.

Write the numbers of quotations which link to this one here ↘

This quotation is from _____.

One poetic technique used is _____.

Another poetic technique used is _____.

The word class of the key word "_____" is _____.

Write the quotation here- make sure it is exactly the same as it is on the other side!

Ask: How does this make you feel?
Ask: How would other audiences feel?
Ask: How does this link to context?

⑥

"Mind-forged Manacles."

FLASHCARD

TEAR THIS PAGE OUT, FILL THIS SIDE IN AND BINGO! YOU HAVE A FABULOUS FLASHCARD.

WRITE THE NUMBERS OF QUOTATIONS WHICH LINK TO THIS ONE HERE ↘

THIS QUOTATION IS FROM
_____ .

ONE POETIC TECHNIQUE USED IS
_____ .

ANOTHER POETIC TECHNIQUE USED IS
_____ .

THE WORD CLASS OF THE KEY WORD "_____" IS _____ .

WRITE THE QUOTATION HERE — MAKE SURE IT IS EXACTLY THE SAME AS IT IS ON THE OTHER SIDE!

ASK: HOW DOES THIS MAKE YOU FEEL?
ASK: HOW WOULD OTHER AUDIENCES FEEL?
ASK: HOW DOES THIS LINK TO CONTEXT?

"Every black'ning church appalls."

FLASHCARD

TEAR THIS PAGE OUT, FILL THIS SIDE IN AND BINGO! YOU HAVE A FABULOUS FLASHCARD.

WRITE THE NUMBERS OF QUOTATIONS WHICH LINK TO THIS ONE HERE ↴

THIS QUOTATION IS FROM
_____.

ONE POETIC TECHNIQUE USED IS
_____.

ANOTHER POETIC TECHNIQUE USED IS
_____.

THE WORD CLASS OF THE KEY WORD "_____"
IS _____.

WRITE THE QUOTATION HERE- MAKE SURE IT IS EXACTLY THE SAME AS IT IS ON THE OTHER SIDE!

ASK: HOW DOES THIS MAKE YOU FEEL?
ASK: HOW WOULD OTHER AUDIENCES FEEL?
ASK: HOW DOES THIS LINK TO CONTEXT?

Pick your own quotation... ⑧

...and do a doodle to suit it.

FLASHCARD

TEAR THIS PAGE OUT, FILL THIS SIDE IN AND BINGO! YOU HAVE A FABULOUS FLASHCARD.

WRITE THE NUMBERS OF QUOTATIONS WHICH LINK TO THIS ONE HERE ↓

THIS QUOTATION IS FROM

_____.

ONE POETIC TECHNIQUE USED IS

_____.

ANOTHER POETIC TECHNIQUE USED IS

_____.

THE WORD CLASS OF THE KEY WORD "_____"

IS _____.

WRITE THE QUOTATION HERE- MAKE SURE IT IS EXACTLY THE SAME AS IT IS ON THE OTHER SIDE!

ASK: HOW DOES THIS MAKE YOU FEEL?

ASK: HOW WOULD OTHER AUDIENCES FEEL?

ASK: HOW DOES THIS LINK TO CONTEXT?

"My boat / Went heaving through the water like a swan."

FLASHCARD

Tear this page out, fill this side in and BINGO! You have a fabulous flashcard.

Write the numbers of quotations which link to this one here ↓

This quotation is from _____.

One poetic technique used is _____.

Another poetic technique used is _____.

The word class of the key word "_____" is _____.

Write the quotation here- make sure it is exactly the same as it is on the other side!

Ask: How does this make you feel?
Ask: How would other audiences feel?
Ask: How does this link to context?

"A huge peak, black and huge, / As if with voluntary power instinct, / Upreared its head."

FLASHCARD

TEAR THIS PAGE OUT, FILL THIS SIDE IN AND BINGO! YOU HAVE A FABULOUS FLASHCARD.

WRITE THE NUMBERS OF QUOTATIONS WHICH LINK TO THIS ONE HERE ↘

THIS QUOTATION IS FROM

_____.

ONE POETIC TECHNIQUE USED IS

_____.

ANOTHER POETIC TECHNIQUE USED IS

_____.

THE WORD CLASS OF THE KEY WORD "_____"

IS _____.

WRITE THE QUOTATION HERE - MAKE SURE IT IS EXACTLY THE SAME AS IT IS ON THE OTHER SIDE!

ASK: HOW DOES THIS MAKE YOU FEEL?
ASK: HOW WOULD OTHER AUDIENCES FEEL?
ASK: HOW DOES THIS LINK TO CONTEXT?

⑪

"O'er my thoughts / There hung a darkness, call it solitude."

FLASHCARD

Tear this page out, fill this side in and bingo! You have a fabulous flashcard.

Write the numbers of quotations which link to this one here ↘

This quotation is from
_____.

One poetic technique used is
_____.

Another poetic technique used is
_____.

The word class of the key word "_____" is _____.

Write the quotation here - make sure it is exactly the same as it is on the other side!

Ask: How does this make you feel?
Ask: How would other audiences feel?
Ask: How does this link to context?

Pick your own quotation...

...and do a doodle to suit it.

FLASHCARD

TEAR THIS PAGE OUT, FILL THIS SIDE IN AND BINGO! YOU HAVE A FABULOUS FLASHCARD.

WRITE THE NUMBERS OF QUOTATIONS WHICH LINK TO THIS ONE HERE ↘

THIS QUOTATION IS FROM
_____.

ONE POETIC TECHNIQUE USED IS
_____.

ANOTHER POETIC TECHNIQUE USED IS
_____.

THE WORD CLASS OF THE KEY WORD "_____"
IS _____.

WRITE THE QUOTATION HERE- MAKE SURE IT IS EXACTLY THE SAME AS IT IS ON THE OTHER SIDE!

ASK: HOW DOES THIS MAKE YOU FEEL?
ASK: HOW WOULD OTHER AUDIENCES FEEL?
ASK: HOW DOES THIS LINK TO CONTEXT?

⑬

"Sir, 'twas not/ Her husband's presence only, called that spot/ Of joy into the Duchess' cheek."

FLASHCARD

TEAR THIS PAGE OUT, FILL THIS SIDE IN AND BINGO! YOU HAVE A FABULOUS FLASHCARD.

WRITE THE NUMBERS OF QUOTATIONS WHICH LINK TO THIS ONE HERE ↘

THIS QUOTATION IS FROM
_____.

ONE POETIC TECHNIQUE USED IS
_____.

ANOTHER POETIC TECHNIQUE USED IS
_____.

THE WORD CLASS OF THE KEY WORD "_____"
IS _____.

WRITE THE QUOTATION HERE – MAKE SURE IT IS EXACTLY THE SAME AS IT IS ON THE OTHER SIDE!

ASK: HOW DOES THIS MAKE YOU FEEL?
ASK: HOW WOULD OTHER AUDIENCES FEEL?
ASK: HOW DOES THIS LINK TO CONTEXT?

"She had / A heart — how shall I say? — too soon made glad."

⑭

FLASHCARD

TEAR THIS PAGE OUT, FILL THIS SIDE IN AND BINGO! YOU HAVE A FABULOUS FLASHCARD.

WRITE THE NUMBERS OF QUOTATIONS WHICH LINK TO THIS ONE HERE ↓

THIS QUOTATION IS FROM
_____.

ONE POETIC TECHNIQUE USED IS
_____.

ANOTHER POETIC TECHNIQUE USED IS
_____.

THE WORD CLASS OF THE KEY WORD "_____"
IS _____.

WRITE THE QUOTATION HERE- MAKE SURE IT IS EXACTLY THE SAME AS IT IS ON THE OTHER SIDE!

ASK: HOW DOES THIS MAKE YOU FEEL?
ASK: HOW WOULD OTHER AUDIENCES FEEL?
ASK: HOW DOES THIS LINK TO CONTEXT?

"I gave commands;/ Then all smiles stopped together."

FLASHCARD

TEAR THIS PAGE OUT, FILL THIS SIDE IN AND BINGO! YOU HAVE A FABULOUS FLASHCARD.

WRITE THE NUMBERS OF QUOTATIONS WHICH LINK TO THIS ONE HERE ↘

THIS QUOTATION IS FROM

_____●

ONE POETIC TECHNIQUE USED IS

_____●

ANOTHER POETIC TECHNIQUE USED IS

_____●

THE WORD CLASS OF THE KEY WORD "_____"

IS _____●

WRITE THE QUOTATION HERE - MAKE SURE IT IS EXACTLY THE SAME AS IT IS ON THE OTHER SIDE!

ASK: HOW DOES THIS MAKE YOU FEEL?

ASK: HOW WOULD OTHER AUDIENCES FEEL?

ASK: HOW DOES THIS LINK TO CONTEXT?

Pick your own quotation... (16)

...and do a doodle to suit it.

FLASHCARD

Tear this page out, fill this side in and bingo! You have a fabulous flashcard.

Write the numbers of quotations which link to this one here ↘

This quotation is from _____.

One poetic technique used is _____.

Another poetic technique used is _____.

The word class of the key word "_____" is _____.

Write the quotation here- make sure it is exactly the same as it is on the other side!

Ask: How does this make you feel?
Ask: How would other audiences feel?
Ask: How does this link to context?

"'Forward, the Light Brigade!'/
Was there a man dismayed?"

17

FLASHCARD

Tear this page out, fill this side in and bingo! You have a fabulous flashcard.

Write the numbers of quotations which link to this one here ↘

This quotation is from _____.

One poetic technique used is _____.

Another poetic technique used is _____.

The word class of the key word "_____" is _____.

Write the quotation here — make sure it is exactly the same as it is on the other side!

Ask: How does this make you feel?
Ask: How would other audiences feel?
Ask: How does this link to context?

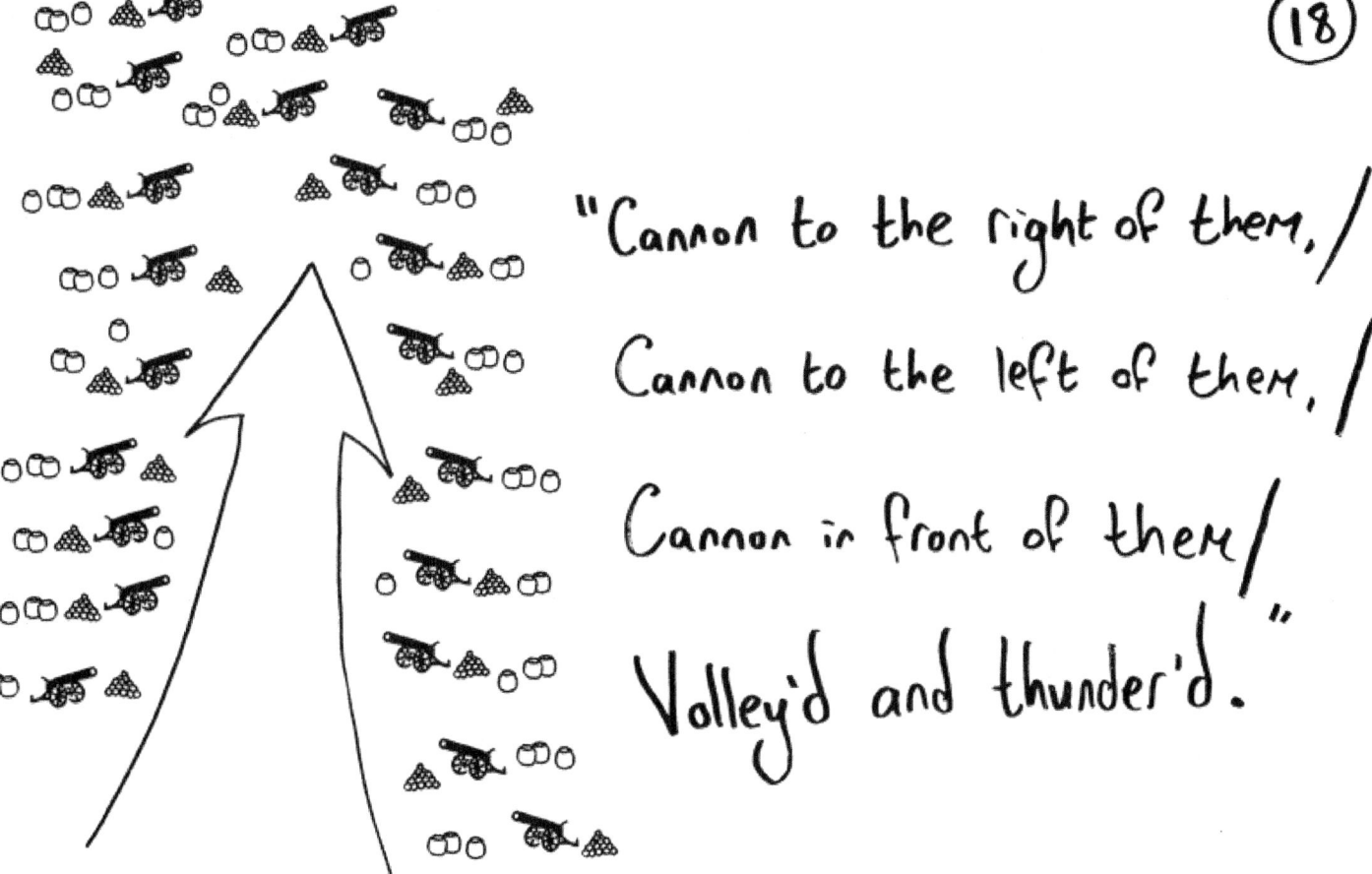

"Cannon to the right of them, / Cannon to the left of them, / Cannon in front of them / Volley'd and thunder'd."

FLASHCARD

Tear this page out, fill this side in and bingo! You have a fabulous flashcard.

Write the numbers of quotations which link to this one here ↓

This quotation is from _____.

One poetic technique used is _____.

Another poetic technique used is _____.

The word class of the key word "_____" is _____.

Write the quotation here - make sure it is exactly the same as it is on the other side!

Ask: How does this make you feel?
Ask: How would other audiences feel?
Ask: How does this link to context?

"When can their glory fade?"

⑲

FLASHCARD

TEAR THIS PAGE OUT, FILL THIS SIDE IN AND BINGO! YOU HAVE A FABULOUS FLASHCARD.

WRITE THE NUMBERS OF QUOTATIONS WHICH LINK TO THIS ONE HERE ↘

THIS QUOTATION IS FROM

_____ .

ONE POETIC TECHNIQUE USED IS

_____ .

ANOTHER POETIC TECHNIQUE USED IS

_____ .

THE WORD CLASS OF THE KEY WORD "_____" IS _____ .

WRITE THE QUOTATION HERE- MAKE SURE IT IS EXACTLY THE SAME AS IT IS ON THE OTHER SIDE!

ASK: HOW DOES THIS MAKE YOU FEEL?
ASK: HOW WOULD OTHER AUDIENCES FEEL?
ASK: HOW DOES THIS LINK TO CONTEXT?

Pick your own quotation... [20]

...and do a doodle to suit it.

FLASHCARD

TEAR THIS PAGE OUT, FILL THIS SIDE IN AND BINGO! YOU HAVE A FABULOUS FLASHCARD.

WRITE THE NUMBERS OF QUOTATIONS WHICH LINK TO THIS ONE HERE ↴

THIS QUOTATION IS FROM
_____.

ONE POETIC TECHNIQUE USED IS
_____.

ANOTHER POETIC TECHNIQUE USED IS
_____.

THE WORD CLASS OF THE KEY WORD "_____"
IS _____.

WRITE THE QUOTATION HERE- MAKE SURE IT IS EXACTLY THE SAME AS IT IS ON THE OTHER SIDE!

ASK: HOW DOES THIS MAKE YOU FEEL?
ASK: HOW WOULD OTHER AUDIENCES FEEL?
ASK: HOW DOES THIS LINK TO CONTEXT?

"The flickering gunnery rumbles, / Far off, like a dull rumour of some other war."

FLASHCARD

TEAR THIS PAGE OUT, FILL THIS SIDE IN AND BINGO! YOU HAVE A FABULOUS FLASHCARD.

WRITE THE NUMBERS OF QUOTATIONS WHICH LINK TO THIS ONE HERE ↘

THIS QUOTATION IS FROM
_____ .

ONE POETIC TECHNIQUE USED IS
_____ .

ANOTHER POETIC TECHNIQUE USED IS
_____ .

THE WORD CLASS OF THE KEY WORD "_____"
IS _____ .

WRITE THE QUOTATION HERE— MAKE SURE IT IS EXACTLY THE SAME AS IT IS ON THE OTHER SIDE!

ASK: HOW DOES THIS MAKE YOU FEEL?
ASK: HOW WOULD OTHER AUDIENCES FEEL?
ASK: HOW DOES THIS LINK TO CONTEXT?

"Sudden successive flights of bullets streak the silence."

(22)

FLASHCARD

TEAR THIS PAGE OUT, FILL THIS SIDE IN AND BINGO! YOU HAVE A FABULOUS FLASHCARD.

WRITE THE NUMBERS OF QUOTATIONS WHICH LINK TO THIS ONE HERE ↓

THIS QUOTATION IS FROM

_____.

ONE POETIC TECHNIQUE USED IS

_____.

ANOTHER POETIC TECHNIQUE USED IS

_____.

THE WORD CLASS OF THE KEY WORD "_____" IS _____.

WRITE THE QUOTATION HERE- MAKE SURE IT IS EXACTLY THE SAME AS IT IS ON THE OTHER SIDE!

ASK: HOW DOES THIS MAKE YOU FEEL?
ASK: HOW WOULD OTHER AUDIENCES FEEL?
ASK: HOW DOES THIS LINK TO CONTEXT?

"All their eyes are ice, / But nothing happens."

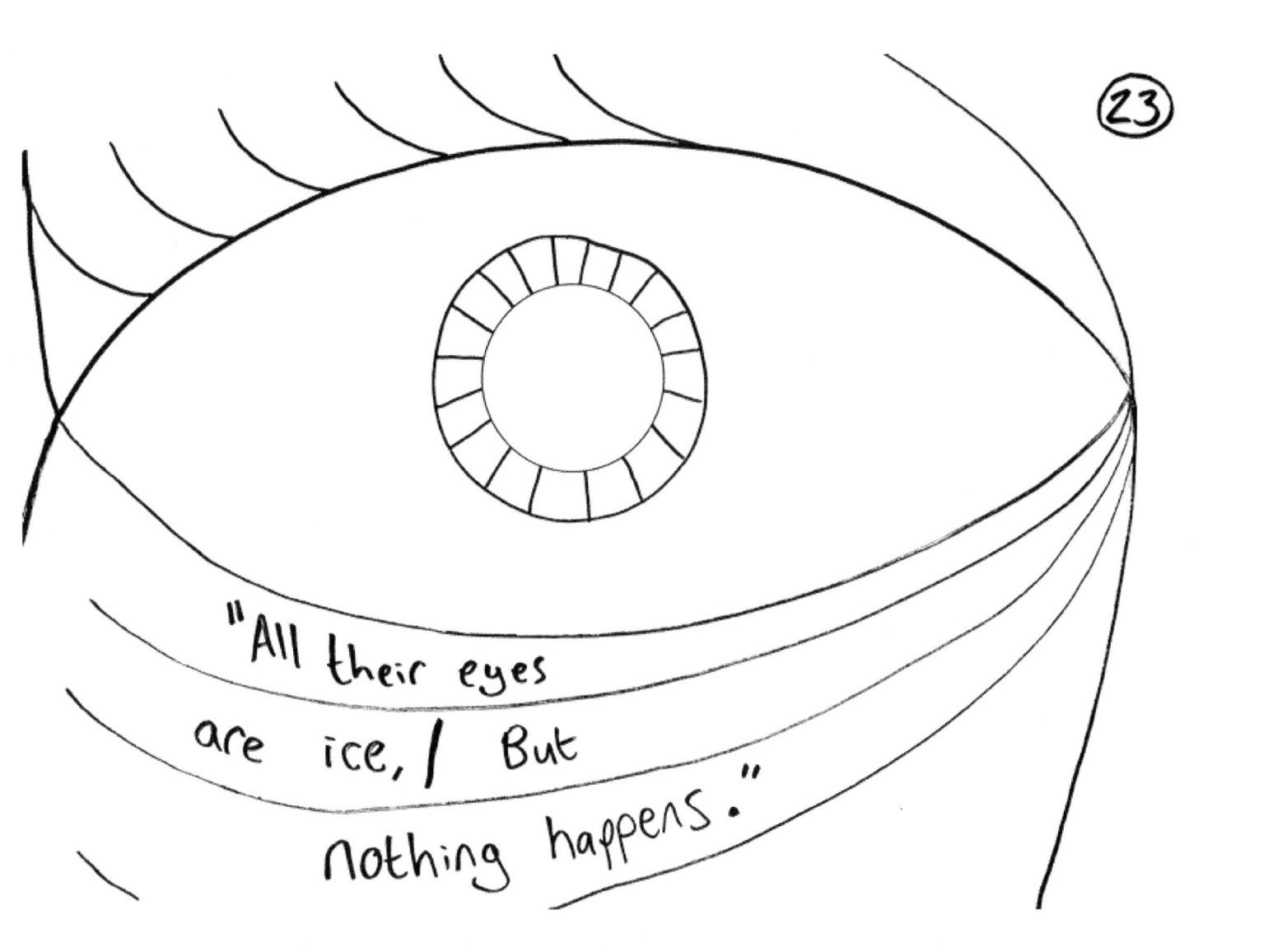

(23)

FLASHCARD

TEAR THIS PAGE OUT, FILL THIS SIDE IN AND BINGO! YOU HAVE A FABULOUS FLASHCARD.

WRITE THE NUMBERS OF QUOTATIONS WHICH LINK TO THIS ONE HERE ↓

THIS QUOTATION IS FROM

_____ .

ONE POETIC TECHNIQUE USED IS

_____ .

ANOTHER POETIC TECHNIQUE USED IS

_____ .

THE WORD CLASS OF THE KEY WORD "_____" IS _____ .

WRITE THE QUOTATION HERE- MAKE SURE IT IS EXACTLY THE SAME AS IT IS ON THE OTHER SIDE!

ASK: HOW DOES THIS MAKE YOU FEEL?
ASK: HOW WOULD OTHER AUDIENCES FEEL?
ASK: HOW DOES THIS LINK TO CONTEXT?

Pick your own quotation...

(24)

...and do a doodle to suit it.

FLASHCARD

TEAR THIS PAGE OUT, FILL THIS SIDE IN AND BINGO! YOU HAVE A FABULOUS FLASHCARD.

WRITE THE NUMBERS OF QUOTATIONS WHICH LINK TO THIS ONE HERE ↙

THIS QUOTATION IS FROM _____.

ONE POETIC TECHNIQUE USED IS _____.

ANOTHER POETIC TECHNIQUE USED IS _____.

THE WORD CLASS OF THE KEY WORD "_____" IS _____.

WRITE THE QUOTATION HERE- MAKE SURE IT IS EXACTLY THE SAME AS IT IS ON THE OTHER SIDE!

ASK: HOW DOES THIS MAKE YOU FEEL?
ASK: HOW WOULD OTHER AUDIENCES FEEL?
ASK: HOW DOES THIS LINK TO CONTEXT?

"We are prepared: we build our houses squat,/ Sink walls in rock and roof them with good slate."

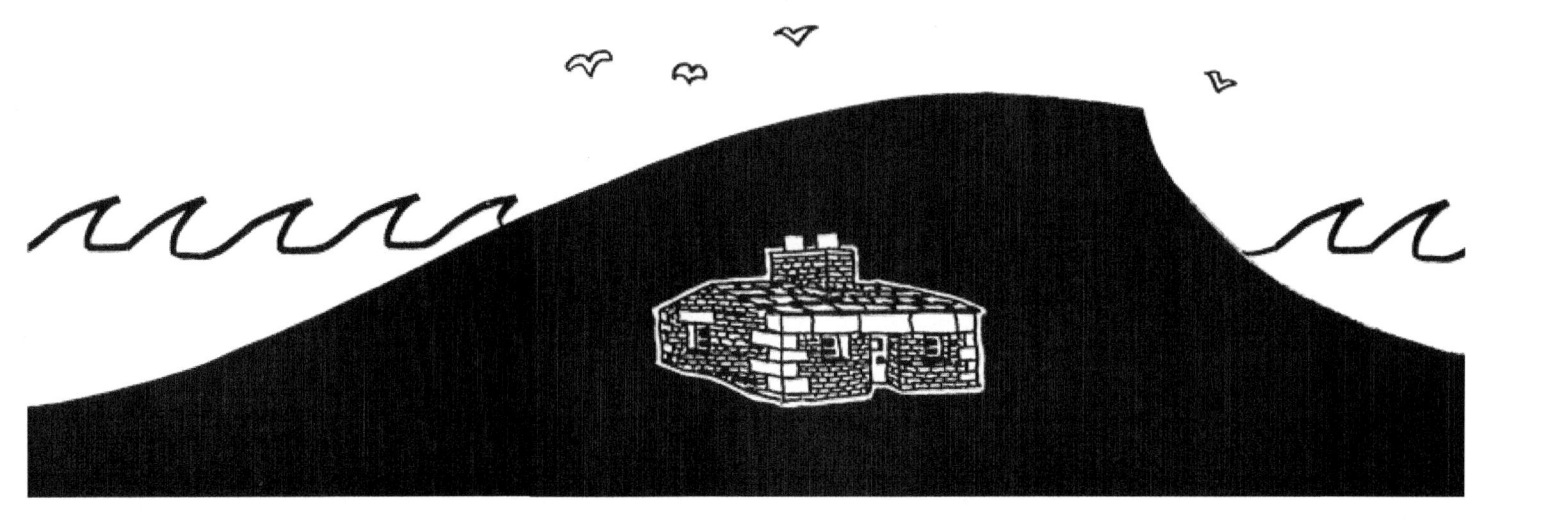

FLASHCARD

TEAR THIS PAGE OUT, FILL THIS SIDE IN AND BINGO! YOU HAVE A FABULOUS FLASHCARD.

WRITE THE NUMBERS OF QUOTATIONS WHICH LINK TO THIS ONE HERE ↘

THIS QUOTATION IS FROM _____.

ONE POETIC TECHNIQUE USED IS _____.

ANOTHER POETIC TECHNIQUE USED IS _____.

THE WORD CLASS OF THE KEY WORD "_____" IS _____.

WRITE THE QUOTATION HERE- MAKE SURE IT IS EXACTLY THE SAME AS IT IS ON THE OTHER SIDE!

ASK: HOW DOES THIS MAKE YOU FEEL?
ASK: HOW WOULD OTHER AUDIENCES FEEL?
ASK: HOW DOES THIS LINK TO CONTEXT?

"Spits like a tame cat / Turned savage."

FLASHCARD

Tear this page out, fill this side in and bingo! You have a fabulous flashcard.

Write the numbers of quotations which link to this one here ⬇

This quotation is from
_____ •

One poetic technique used is
_____ •

Another poetic technique used is
_____ •

The word class of the key word "_____" is _____ •

Write the quotation here- make sure it is exactly the same as it is on the other side!

ASK: How does this make you feel?
ASK: How would other audiences feel?
ASK: How does this link to context?

"We are bombarded by the empty air."

(27)

FLASHCARD

TEAR THIS PAGE OUT, FILL THIS SIDE IN AND BINGO! YOU HAVE A FABULOUS FLASHCARD.

WRITE THE NUMBERS OF QUOTATIONS WHICH LINK TO THIS ONE HERE ↘

THIS QUOTATION IS FROM

_____ •

ONE POETIC TECHNIQUE USED IS

_____ •

ANOTHER POETIC TECHNIQUE USED IS

_____ •

THE WORD CLASS OF THE KEY WORD "_____"

IS _____ •

WRITE THE QUOTATION HERE- MAKE SURE IT IS EXACTLY THE SAME AS IT IS ON THE OTHER SIDE!

ASK: HOW DOES THIS MAKE YOU FEEL?
ASK: HOW WOULD OTHER AUDIENCES FEEL?
ASK: HOW DOES THIS LINK TO CONTEXT?

Pick your own quotation... (28)

...and do a doodle to suit it.

FLASHCARD

TEAR THIS PAGE OUT, FILL THIS SIDE IN AND BINGO! YOU HAVE A FABULOUS FLASHCARD.

WRITE THE NUMBERS OF QUOTATIONS WHICH LINK TO THIS ONE HERE ↓

THIS QUOTATION IS FROM _____.

ONE POETIC TECHNIQUE USED IS _____.

ANOTHER POETIC TECHNIQUE USED IS _____.

THE WORD CLASS OF THE KEY WORD "_____" IS _____.

WRITE THE QUOTATION HERE— MAKE SURE IT IS EXACTLY THE SAME AS IT IS ON THE OTHER SIDE!

ASK: HOW DOES THIS MAKE YOU FEEL?
ASK: HOW WOULD OTHER AUDIENCES FEEL?
ASK: HOW DOES THIS LINK TO CONTEXT?

(29)

"He lugged a rifle numb as a smashed arm."

FLASHCARD

TEAR THIS PAGE OUT, FILL THIS SIDE IN AND BINGO! YOU HAVE A FABULOUS FLASHCARD.

WRITE THE NUMBERS OF QUOTATIONS WHICH LINK TO THIS ONE HERE ↘

THIS QUOTATION IS FROM

_____ •

ONE POETIC TECHNIQUE USED IS

_____ •

ANOTHER POETIC TECHNIQUE USED IS

_____ •

THE WORD CLASS OF THE KEY WORD "_____"

IS _____ •

WRITE THE QUOTATION HERE - MAKE SURE IT IS EXACTLY THE SAME AS IT IS ON THE OTHER SIDE!

ASK: HOW DOES THIS MAKE YOU FEEL?
ASK: HOW WOULD OTHER AUDIENCES FEEL?
ASK: HOW DOES THIS LINK TO CONTEXT?

(30)

"In what cold clockwork of the stars and the nations/ Was he the hand pointing that second?"

Hughes

FLASHCARD

Tear this page out, fill this side in and bingo! You have a fabulous flashcard.

Write the numbers of quotations which link to this one here ↓

This quotation is from _____.

One poetic technique used is _____.

Another poetic technique used is _____.

The word class of the key word "_____" is _____.

Write the quotation here - make sure it is exactly the same as it is on the other side!

ASK: How does this make you feel?
ASK: How would other audiences feel?
ASK: How does this link to context?

"His foot hung like statuary in mid-stride."

FLASHCARD

TEAR THIS PAGE OUT, FILL THIS SIDE IN AND BINGO! YOU HAVE A FABULOUS FLASHCARD.

WRITE THE NUMBERS OF QUOTATIONS WHICH LINK TO THIS ONE HERE ➔

THIS QUOTATION IS FROM
_____ •

ONE POETIC TECHNIQUE USED IS
_____ •

ANOTHER POETIC TECHNIQUE USED IS
_____ •

THE WORD CLASS OF THE KEY WORD "_____"
IS _____ •

WRITE THE QUOTATION HERE - MAKE SURE IT IS EXACTLY THE SAME AS IT IS ON THE OTHER SIDE!

ASK: HOW DOES THIS MAKE YOU FEEL?
ASK: HOW WOULD OTHER AUDIENCES FEEL?
ASK: HOW DOES THIS LINK TO CONTEXT?

Pick your own quotation... (32)

...and do a doodle to suit it.

FLASHCARD

Tear this page out, fill this side in and bingo! You have a fabulous flashcard.

Write the numbers of quotations which link to this one here ↓

This quotation is from _____.

One poetic technique used is _____.

Another poetic technique used is _____.

The word class of the key word "_____" is _____.

Write the quotation here - make sure it is exactly the same as it is on the other side!

Ask: How does this make you feel?
Ask: How would other audiences feel?
Ask: How does this link to context?

33

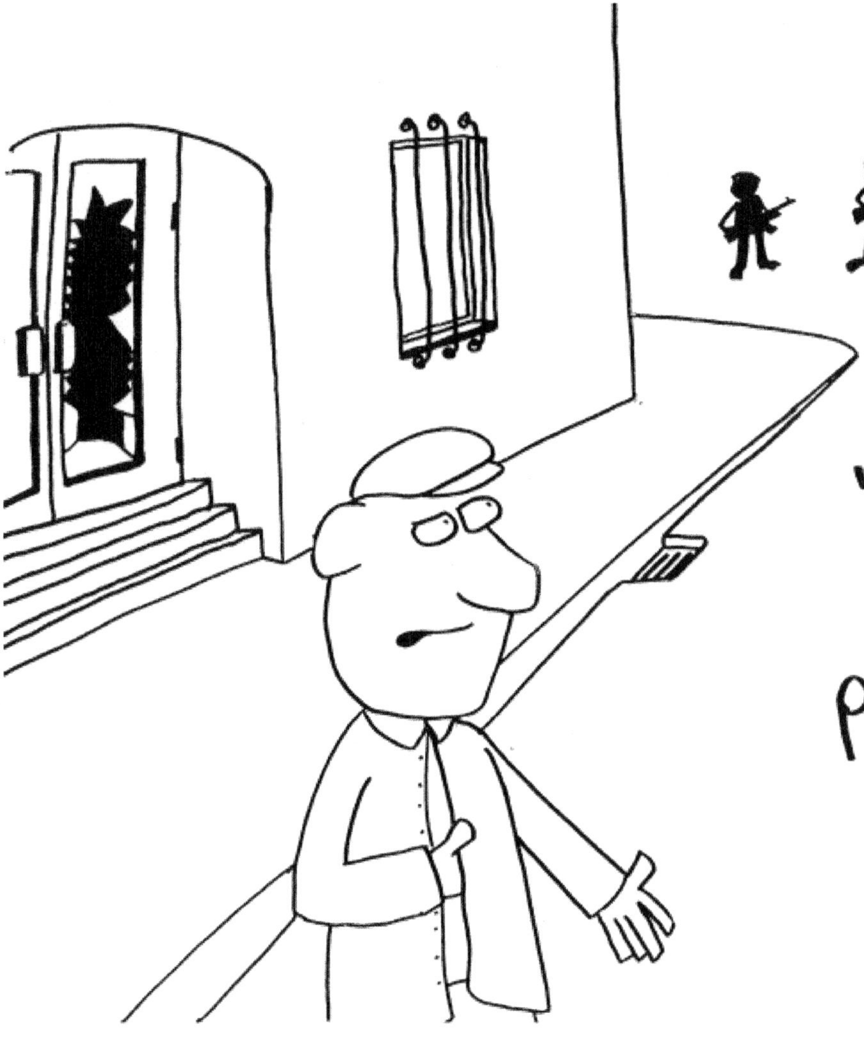

"Probably armed,
possibly not."

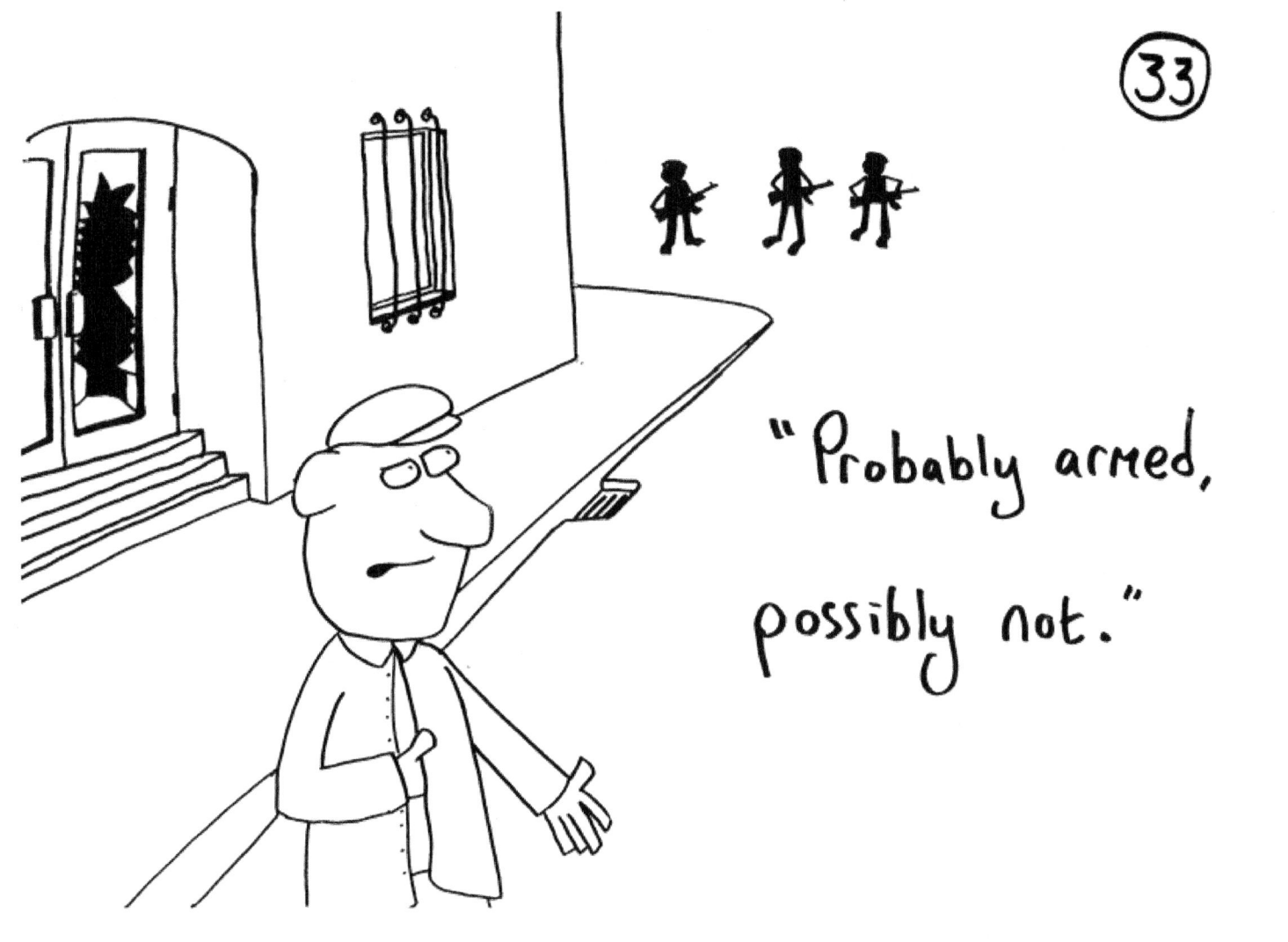

FLASHCARD

TEAR THIS PAGE OUT, FILL THIS SIDE IN AND BINGO! YOU HAVE A FABULOUS FLASHCARD.

WRITE THE NUMBERS OF QUOTATIONS WHICH LINK TO THIS ONE HERE ↴

THIS QUOTATION IS FROM
_____ •

ONE POETIC TECHNIQUE USED IS
_____ •

ANOTHER POETIC TECHNIQUE USED IS
_____ •

THE WORD CLASS OF THE KEY WORD "_____"
IS _____ •

WRITE THE QUOTATION HERE - MAKE SURE IT IS EXACTLY THE SAME AS IT IS ON THE OTHER SIDE!

ASK: HOW DOES THIS MAKE YOU FEEL?
ASK: HOW WOULD OTHER AUDIENCES FEEL?
ASK: HOW DOES THIS LINK TO CONTEXT?

(34)

"I see every round as it rips through his life — / I see broad daylight on the other side."

FLASHCARD

TEAR THIS PAGE OUT, FILL THIS SIDE IN AND BINGO! YOU HAVE A FABULOUS FLASHCARD.

WRITE THE NUMBERS OF QUOTATIONS WHICH LINK TO THIS ONE HERE ↙

THIS QUOTATION IS FROM
_____.

ONE POETIC TECHNIQUE USED IS
_____.

ANOTHER POETIC TECHNIQUE USED IS
_____.

THE WORD CLASS OF THE KEY WORD "_____"
IS _____.

WRITE THE QUOTATION HERE — MAKE SURE IT IS EXACTLY THE SAME AS IT IS ON THE OTHER SIDE!

ASK: HOW DOES THIS MAKE YOU FEEL?
ASK: HOW WOULD OTHER AUDIENCES FEEL?
ASK: HOW DOES THIS LINK TO CONTEXT?

"And the drink and the drugs won't flush him out."

35

FLASHCARD

TEAR THIS PAGE OUT, FILL THIS SIDE IN AND BINGO! YOU HAVE A FABULOUS FLASHCARD.

WRITE THE NUMBERS OF QUOTATIONS WHICH LINK TO THIS ONE HERE ↴

THIS QUOTATION IS FROM _____.

ONE POETIC TECHNIQUE USED IS _____.

ANOTHER POETIC TECHNIQUE USED IS _____.

THE WORD CLASS OF THE KEY WORD "_____" IS _____.

WRITE THE QUOTATION HERE- MAKE SURE IT IS EXACTLY THE SAME AS IT IS ON THE OTHER SIDE!

ASK: HOW DOES THIS MAKE YOU FEEL?
ASK: HOW WOULD OTHER AUDIENCES FEEL?
ASK: HOW DOES THIS LINK TO CONTEXT?

Pick your own quotation...

(36)

...and do a doodle to suit it.

FLASHCARD

Tear this page out, fill this side in and bingo! You have a fabulous flashcard.

Write the numbers of quotations which link to this one here ↓

This quotation is from _____.

One poetic technique used is _____.

Another poetic technique used is _____.

The word class of the key word "_____" is _____.

Write the quotation here- make sure it is exactly the same as it is on the other side!

Ask: How does this make you feel?
Ask: How would other audiences feel?
Ask: How does this link to context?

"I resisted the impulse to run my fingers through the gelled blackthorns of your hair."

37

FLASHCARD

TEAR THIS PAGE OUT, FILL THIS SIDE IN AND BINGO! YOU HAVE A FABULOUS FLASHCARD.

WRITE THE NUMBERS OF QUOTATIONS WHICH LINK TO THIS ONE HERE ↓

THIS QUOTATION IS FROM
_____ •

ONE POETIC TECHNIQUE USED IS
_____ •

ANOTHER POETIC TECHNIQUE USED IS
_____ •

THE WORD CLASS OF THE KEY WORD "_____"
IS _____ •

WRITE THE QUOTATION HERE - MAKE SURE IT IS EXACTLY THE SAME AS IT IS ON THE OTHER SIDE!

ASK: HOW DOES THIS MAKE YOU FEEL?
ASK: HOW WOULD OTHER AUDIENCES FEEL?
ASK: HOW DOES THIS LINK TO CONTEXT?

38

"After you'd gone I went into your bedroom, I released a song bird from its cage."

FLASHCARD

TEAR THIS PAGE OUT, FILL THIS SIDE IN AND BINGO! YOU HAVE A FABULOUS FLASHCARD.

WRITE THE NUMBERS OF QUOTATIONS WHICH LINK TO THIS ONE HERE ↴

THIS QUOTATION IS FROM
_____

ONE POETIC TECHNIQUE USED IS
_____

ANOTHER POETIC TECHNIQUE USED IS
_____

THE WORD CLASS OF THE KEY WORD "_____" IS _____

WRITE THE QUOTATION HERE - MAKE SURE IT IS EXACTLY THE SAME AS IT IS ON THE OTHER SIDE!

ASK: HOW DOES THIS MAKE YOU FEEL?
ASK: HOW WOULD OTHER AUDIENCES FEEL?
ASK: HOW DOES THIS LINK TO CONTEXT?

(39)

"On reaching the top of the hill I traced / the inscriptions on the war memorial, / leaned against it like a wishbone."

FLASHCARD

TEAR THIS PAGE OUT, FILL THIS SIDE IN AND BINGO! YOU HAVE A FABULOUS FLASHCARD.

WRITE THE NUMBERS OF QUOTATIONS WHICH LINK TO THIS ONE HERE ⬇

THIS QUOTATION IS FROM

_____•

ONE POETIC TECHNIQUE USED IS

_____•

ANOTHER POETIC TECHNIQUE USED IS

_____•

THE WORD CLASS OF THE KEY WORD "_____"

IS _____•

WRITE THE QUOTATION HERE- MAKE SURE IT IS EXACTLY THE SAME AS IT IS ON THE OTHER SIDE!

ASK: HOW DOES THIS MAKE YOU FEEL?

ASK: HOW WOULD OTHER AUDIENCES FEEL?

ASK: HOW DOES THIS LINK TO CONTEXT?

Pick your own quotation...

(40)

...and do a doodle to suit it.

FLASHCARD

TEAR THIS PAGE OUT, FILL THIS SIDE IN AND BINGO! YOU HAVE A FABULOUS FLASHCARD.

WRITE THE NUMBERS OF QUOTATIONS WHICH LINK TO THIS ONE HERE ↓

THIS QUOTATION IS FROM
_____.

ONE POETIC TECHNIQUE USED IS
_____.

ANOTHER POETIC TECHNIQUE USED IS
_____.

THE WORD CLASS OF THE KEY WORD "_____"
IS _____.

WRITE THE QUOTATION HERE- MAKE SURE IT IS EXACTLY THE SAME AS IT IS ON THE OTHER SIDE!

ASK: HOW DOES THIS MAKE YOU FEEL?
ASK: HOW WOULD OTHER AUDIENCES FEEL?
ASK: HOW DOES THIS LINK TO CONTEXT?

(41)

"Belfast. Beirut. Phnom Penh.

All flesh is grass."

FLASHCARD

TEAR THIS PAGE OUT, FILL THIS SIDE IN AND BINGO! YOU HAVE A FABULOUS FLASHCARD.

WRITE THE NUMBERS OF QUOTATIONS WHICH LINK TO THIS ONE HERE ↘

THIS QUOTATION IS FROM
_____.

ONE POETIC TECHNIQUE USED IS
_____.

ANOTHER POETIC TECHNIQUE USED IS
_____.

THE WORD CLASS OF THE KEY WORD "_____"
IS _____.

WRITE THE QUOTATION HERE- MAKE SURE IT IS EXACTLY THE SAME AS IT IS ON THE OTHER SIDE!

ASK: HOW DOES THIS MAKE YOU FEEL?
ASK: HOW WOULD OTHER AUDIENCES FEEL?
ASK: HOW DOES THIS LINK TO CONTEXT?

"A hundred agonies in black-and-white."

FLASHCARD

Tear this page out, fill this side in and BINGO! You have a fabulous flashcard.

Write the numbers of quotations which link to this one here ↓

This quotation is from _____.

One poetic technique used is _____.

Another poetic technique used is _____.

The word class of the key word "_____" is _____.

Write the quotation here— make sure it is exactly the same as it is on the other side!

Ask: How does this make you feel?
Ask: How would other audiences feel?
Ask: How does this link to context?

"The reader's eyeballs prick with tears between the bath and the pre-lunch beers."

FLASHCARD

TEAR THIS PAGE OUT, FILL THIS SIDE IN AND BINGO! YOU HAVE A FABULOUS FLASHCARD.

WRITE THE NUMBERS OF QUOTATIONS WHICH LINK TO THIS ONE HERE ↓

THIS QUOTATION IS FROM
_____.

ONE POETIC TECHNIQUE USED IS
_____.

ANOTHER POETIC TECHNIQUE USED IS
_____.

THE WORD CLASS OF THE KEY WORD "_____"
IS _____.

WRITE THE QUOTATION HERE- MAKE SURE IT IS EXACTLY THE SAME AS IT IS ON THE OTHER SIDE!

ASK: HOW DOES THIS MAKE YOU FEEL?
ASK: HOW WOULD OTHER AUDIENCES FEEL?
ASK: HOW DOES THIS LINK TO CONTEXT?

Pick your own quotation...

(44)

...and do a doodle to suit it.

FLASHCARD

TEAR THIS PAGE OUT, FILL THIS SIDE IN AND BINGO! YOU HAVE A FABULOUS FLASHCARD.

WRITE THE NUMBERS OF QUOTATIONS WHICH LINK TO THIS ONE HERE ↓

THIS QUOTATION IS FROM
_____.

ONE POETIC TECHNIQUE USED IS
_____.

ANOTHER POETIC TECHNIQUE USED IS
_____.

THE WORD CLASS OF THE KEY WORD "_____"
IS _____.

WRITE THE QUOTATION HERE— MAKE SURE IT IS EXACTLY THE SAME AS IT IS ON THE OTHER SIDE!

ASK: HOW DOES THIS MAKE YOU FEEL?
ASK: HOW WOULD OTHER AUDIENCES FEEL?
ASK: HOW DOES THIS LINK TO CONTEXT?

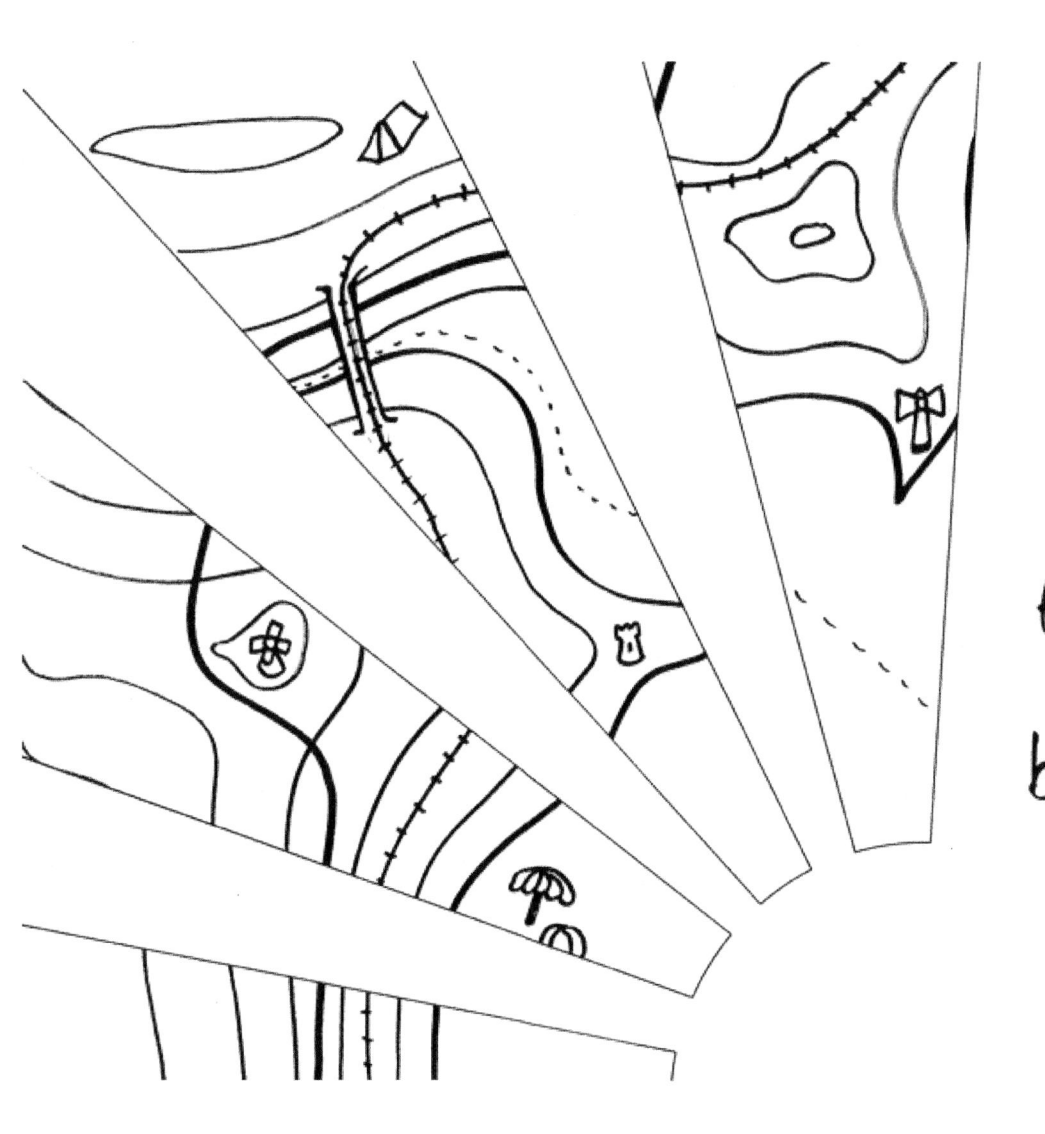

"Maps too. The sun shines through/their borderlines."

45

FLASHCARD

TEAR THIS PAGE OUT, FILL THIS SIDE IN AND BINGO! YOU HAVE A FABULOUS FLASHCARD.

WRITE THE NUMBERS OF QUOTATIONS WHICH LINK TO THIS ONE HERE ↓

THIS QUOTATION IS FROM
_____.

ONE POETIC TECHNIQUE USED IS
_____.

ANOTHER POETIC TECHNIQUE USED IS
_____.

THE WORD CLASS OF THE KEY WORD "_____"
IS _____.

WRITE THE QUOTATION HERE- MAKE SURE IT IS EXACTLY THE SAME AS IT IS ON THE OTHER SIDE!

ASK: HOW DOES THIS MAKE YOU FEEL?
ASK: HOW WOULD OTHER AUDIENCES FEEL?
ASK: HOW DOES THIS LINK TO CONTEXT?

"Fine slips from grocery shops... might fly our lives like paper kites."

FLASHCARD

TEAR THIS PAGE OUT, FILL THIS SIDE IN AND BINGO! YOU HAVE A FABULOUS FLASHCARD.

WRITE THE NUMBERS OF QUOTATIONS WHICH LINK TO THIS ONE HERE ↓

THIS QUOTATION IS FROM

_____ .

ONE POETIC TECHNIQUE USED IS

_____ .

ANOTHER POETIC TECHNIQUE USED IS

_____ .

THE WORD CLASS OF THE KEY WORD "_____"

IS _____ .

WRITE THE QUOTATION HERE - MAKE SURE IT IS EXACTLY THE SAME AS IT IS ON THE OTHER SIDE!

ASK: HOW DOES THIS MAKE YOU FEEL?
ASK: HOW WOULD OTHER AUDIENCES FEEL?
ASK: HOW DOES THIS LINK TO CONTEXT?

"Raise a structure / never meant to last."

(47)

FLASHCARD

TEAR THIS PAGE OUT, FILL THIS SIDE IN AND BINGO! YOU HAVE A FABULOUS FLASHCARD.

WRITE THE NUMBERS OF QUOTATIONS WHICH LINK TO THIS ONE HERE ↙

THIS QUOTATION IS FROM
_____.

ONE POETIC TECHNIQUE USED IS
_____.

ANOTHER POETIC TECHNIQUE USED IS
_____.

THE WORD CLASS OF THE KEY WORD "_____" IS _____.

WRITE THE QUOTATION HERE - MAKE SURE IT IS EXACTLY THE SAME AS IT IS ON THE OTHER SIDE!

ASK: HOW DOES THIS MAKE YOU FEEL?
ASK: HOW WOULD OTHER AUDIENCES FEEL?
ASK: HOW DOES THIS LINK TO CONTEXT?

Pick your own quotation...

(48)

...and do a doodle to suit it.

FLASHCARD

TEAR THIS PAGE OUT, FILL THIS SIDE IN AND BINGO! YOU HAVE A FABULOUS FLASHCARD.

WRITE THE NUMBERS OF QUOTATIONS WHICH LINK TO THIS ONE HERE ↓

THIS QUOTATION IS FROM _____.

ONE POETIC TECHNIQUE USED IS _____

ANOTHER POETIC TECHNIQUE USED IS _____

THE WORD CLASS OF THE KEY WORD "_____" IS _____.

WRITE THE QUOTATION HERE- MAKE SURE IT IS EXACTLY THE SAME AS IT IS ON THE OTHER SIDE!

ASK: HOW DOES THIS MAKE YOU FEEL?
ASK: HOW WOULD OTHER AUDIENCES FEEL?
ASK: HOW DOES THIS LINK TO CONTEXT?

"It may be at war, it may be sick with tyrants."

FLASHCARD

TEAR THIS PAGE OUT, FILL THIS SIDE IN AND BINGO! YOU HAVE A FABULOUS FLASHCARD.

WRITE THE NUMBERS OF QUOTATIONS WHICH LINK TO THIS ONE HERE ⬇

THIS QUOTATION IS FROM

_____ •

ONE POETIC TECHNIQUE USED IS

_____ •

ANOTHER POETIC TECHNIQUE USED IS

_____ •

THE WORD CLASS OF THE KEY WORD "_____"

IS _____ •

WRITE THE QUOTATION HERE - MAKE SURE IT IS EXACTLY THE SAME AS IT IS ON THE OTHER SIDE!

ASK: HOW DOES THIS MAKE YOU FEEL?

ASK: HOW WOULD OTHER AUDIENCES FEEL?

ASK: HOW DOES THIS LINK TO CONTEXT?

"That child's vocabulary I carried here / like a hollow doll, opens and spills a grammar."

FLASHCARD

TEAR THIS PAGE OUT, FILL THIS SIDE IN AND BINGO! YOU HAVE A FABULOUS FLASHCARD.

WRITE THE NUMBERS OF QUOTATIONS WHICH LINK TO THIS ONE HERE ↓

THIS QUOTATION IS FROM
_____.

ONE POETIC TECHNIQUE USED IS
_____.

ANOTHER POETIC TECHNIQUE USED IS
_____.

THE WORD CLASS OF THE KEY WORD "_____"
IS _____.

WRITE THE QUOTATION HERE- MAKE SURE IT IS EXACTLY THE SAME AS IT IS ON THE OTHER SIDE!

ASK: HOW DOES THIS MAKE YOU FEEL?
ASK: HOW WOULD OTHER AUDIENCES FEEL?
ASK: HOW DOES THIS LINK TO CONTEXT?

"My shadow falls as evidence of sunlight."

(51)

FLASHCARD

TEAR THIS PAGE OUT, FILL THIS SIDE IN AND BINGO! YOU HAVE A FABULOUS FLASHCARD.

WRITE THE NUMBERS OF QUOTATIONS WHICH LINK TO THIS ONE HERE ↴

THIS QUOTATION IS FROM

_____ •

ONE POETIC TECHNIQUE USED IS

_____ •

ANOTHER POETIC TECHNIQUE USED IS

_____ •

THE WORD CLASS OF THE KEY WORD "_____"

IS _____ •

WRITE THE QUOTATION HERE- MAKE SURE IT IS EXACTLY THE SAME AS IT IS ON THE OTHER SIDE!

ASK: HOW DOES THIS MAKE YOU FEEL?
ASK: HOW WOULD OTHER AUDIENCES FEEL?
ASK: HOW DOES THIS LINK TO CONTEXT?

Pick your own quotation... (48)

...and do a doodle to suit it.

FLASHCARD

TEAR THIS PAGE OUT, FILL THIS SIDE IN AND BINGO! YOU HAVE A FABULOUS FLASHCARD.

WRITE THE NUMBERS OF QUOTATIONS WHICH LINK TO THIS ONE HERE ↙

THIS QUOTATION IS FROM _____.

ONE POETIC TECHNIQUE USED IS _____.

ANOTHER POETIC TECHNIQUE USED IS _____.

THE WORD CLASS OF THE KEY WORD "_____" IS _____.

WRITE THE QUOTATION HERE- MAKE SURE IT IS EXACTLY THE SAME AS IT IS ON THE OTHER SIDE!

ASK: HOW DOES THIS MAKE YOU FEEL?
ASK: HOW WOULD OTHER AUDIENCES FEEL?
ASK: HOW DOES THIS LINK TO CONTEXT?

"Dem tell me/ Dem tell me/ Wha dem want to tell me."

(53)

FLASHCARD

TEAR THIS PAGE OUT, FILL THIS SIDE IN AND BINGO! YOU HAVE A FABULOUS FLASHCARD.

WRITE THE NUMBERS OF QUOTATIONS WHICH LINK TO THIS ONE HERE ↘

THIS QUOTATION IS FROM

_____ .

ONE POETIC TECHNIQUE USED IS

_____ .

ANOTHER POETIC TECHNIQUE USED IS

_____ .

THE WORD CLASS OF THE KEY WORD "_____" IS _____ .

WRITE THE QUOTATION HERE- MAKE SURE IT IS EXACTLY THE SAME AS IT IS ON THE OTHER SIDE!

ASK: HOW DOES THIS MAKE YOU FEEL?
ASK: HOW WOULD OTHER AUDIENCES FEEL?
ASK: HOW DOES THIS LINK TO CONTEXT?

(54)

"Dem tell me bout Columbus and 1492/
but what happen to de Caribs
and de Arawaks too"

FLASHCARD

TEAR THIS PAGE OUT, FILL THIS SIDE IN AND BINGO! YOU HAVE A FABULOUS FLASHCARD.

WRITE THE NUMBERS OF QUOTATIONS WHICH LINK TO THIS ONE HERE ↓

THIS QUOTATION IS FROM
_____ .

ONE POETIC TECHNIQUE USED IS
_____ .

ANOTHER POETIC TECHNIQUE USED IS
_____ .

THE WORD CLASS OF THE KEY WORD "_____" IS _____ .

WRITE THE QUOTATION HERE- MAKE SURE IT IS EXACTLY THE SAME AS IT IS ON THE OTHER SIDE!

ASK: HOW DOES THIS MAKE YOU FEEL?
ASK: HOW WOULD OTHER AUDIENCES FEEL?
ASK: HOW DOES THIS LINK TO CONTEXT?

"I carving out me identity."

(55)

FLASHCARD

TEAR THIS PAGE OUT, FILL THIS SIDE IN AND BINGO! YOU HAVE A FABULOUS FLASHCARD.

WRITE THE NUMBERS OF QUOTATIONS WHICH LINK TO THIS ONE HERE ↘

THIS QUOTATION IS FROM

_____.

ONE POETIC TECHNIQUE USED IS

_____.

ANOTHER POETIC TECHNIQUE USED IS

_____.

THE WORD CLASS OF THE KEY WORD "_____"

IS _____.

WRITE THE QUOTATION HERE - MAKE SURE IT IS EXACTLY THE SAME AS IT IS ON THE OTHER SIDE!

ASK: HOW DOES THIS MAKE YOU FEEL?

ASK: HOW WOULD OTHER AUDIENCES FEEL?

ASK: HOW DOES THIS LINK TO CONTEXT?

Pick your own quotation...

(56)

...and do a doodle to suit it.

FLASHCARD

TEAR THIS PAGE OUT, FILL THIS SIDE IN AND BINGO! YOU HAVE A FABULOUS FLASHCARD.

WRITE THE NUMBERS OF QUOTATIONS WHICH LINK TO THIS ONE HERE ↘

THIS QUOTATION IS FROM
_____.

ONE POETIC TECHNIQUE USED IS
_____.

ANOTHER POETIC TECHNIQUE USED IS
_____.

THE WORD CLASS OF THE KEY WORD "_____" IS _____.

WRITE THE QUOTATION HERE - MAKE SURE IT IS EXACTLY THE SAME AS IT IS ON THE OTHER SIDE!

ASK: HOW DOES THIS MAKE YOU FEEL?
ASK: HOW WOULD OTHER AUDIENCES FEEL?
ASK: HOW DOES THIS LINK TO CONTEXT?

"He must have looked far down/ at the little fishing boats/ strung out like bunting."

57

FLASHCARD

TEAR THIS PAGE OUT, FILL THIS SIDE IN AND BINGO! YOU HAVE A FABULOUS FLASHCARD.

WRITE THE NUMBERS OF QUOTATIONS WHICH LINK TO THIS ONE HERE ↘

THIS QUOTATION IS FROM
_____ •

ONE POETIC TECHNIQUE USED IS
_____ •

ANOTHER POETIC TECHNIQUE USED IS
_____ •

THE WORD CLASS OF THE KEY WORD "_____" IS _____ •

WRITE THE QUOTATION HERE- MAKE SURE IT IS EXACTLY THE SAME AS IT IS ON THE OTHER SIDE!

ASK: HOW DOES THIS MAKE YOU FEEL?
ASK: HOW WOULD OTHER AUDIENCES FEEL?
ASK: HOW DOES THIS LINK TO CONTEXT?

"And though he came back / my mother never spoke again / in his presence."

58

FLASHCARD

TEAR THIS PAGE OUT, FILL THIS SIDE IN AND BINGO! YOU HAVE A FABULOUS FLASHCARD.

WRITE THE NUMBERS OF QUOTATIONS WHICH LINK TO THIS ONE HERE ↙

THIS QUOTATION IS FROM
_____.

ONE POETIC TECHNIQUE USED IS
_____.

ANOTHER POETIC TECHNIQUE USED IS
_____.

THE WORD CLASS OF THE KEY WORD "_____"
IS _____.

WRITE THE QUOTATION HERE- MAKE SURE IT IS EXACTLY THE SAME AS IT IS ON THE OTHER SIDE!

ASK: HOW DOES THIS MAKE YOU FEEL?
ASK: HOW WOULD OTHER AUDIENCES FEEL?
ASK: HOW DOES THIS LINK TO CONTEXT?

"He must have wondered / which had been the better way to die."

FLASHCARD

TEAR THIS PAGE OUT, FILL THIS SIDE IN AND BINGO! YOU HAVE A FABULOUS FLASHCARD.

WRITE THE NUMBERS OF QUOTATIONS WHICH LINK TO THIS ONE HERE ↴

THIS QUOTATION IS FROM

_____ •

ONE POETIC TECHNIQUE USED IS

_____ •

ANOTHER POETIC TECHNIQUE USED IS

_____ •

THE WORD CLASS OF THE KEY WORD "_____"

IS _____ •

WRITE THE QUOTATION HERE - MAKE SURE IT IS EXACTLY THE SAME AS IT IS ON THE OTHER SIDE!

ASK: HOW DOES THIS MAKE YOU FEEL?

ASK: HOW WOULD OTHER AUDIENCES FEEL?

ASK: HOW DOES THIS LINK TO CONTEXT?

Pick your own quotation... (60)

...and do a doodle to suit it.

FLASHCARD

TEAR THIS PAGE OUT, FILL THIS SIDE IN AND BINGO! YOU HAVE A FABULOUS FLASHCARD.

WRITE THE NUMBERS OF QUOTATIONS WHICH LINK TO THIS ONE HERE ⬇

THIS QUOTATION IS FROM
_____•

ONE POETIC TECHNIQUE USED IS
_____•

ANOTHER POETIC TECHNIQUE USED IS
_____•

THE WORD CLASS OF THE KEY WORD "_____" IS _____•

WRITE THE QUOTATION HERE - MAKE SURE IT IS EXACTLY THE SAME AS IT IS ON THE OTHER SIDE!

ASK: HOW DOES THIS MAKE YOU FEEL?
ASK: HOW WOULD OTHER AUDIENCES FEEL?
ASK: HOW DOES THIS LINK TO CONTEXT?

OF COURSE, NONE OF THIS IS ANY SUBSTITUTE FOR ACTUALLY READING THE POEMS!

With your friends, why not organise a night of poetry reading? Each of you could read a poem — which you'll never ever forget!

Printed in Great Britain
by Amazon